# Terry's Tr
# Samson Strong's
# Shorts

*by Mick Gowar*

Longman

Terry and his class came into the classroom on the first Monday of the summer term. Miss Robinson their teacher wasn't there. Standing in front of the room was a strange man. He was wearing a dark blue blazer with gleaming gold buttons and he had his hands behind his back. He wasn't smiling, like Miss Robinson did. He was scowling. And he was enormous.

The muscles in his arms made the sleeves of his blazer strain, as if they were about to split open. His neck was almost as thick as his head. His wrists looked thicker than Terry's waist. He was built like a motorway bridge, only bigger. And he looked very scary.

When all the class were sitting down, he cracked his knuckles.

"Good morning, boys and girls," he boomed. "My name's Mr Stone. Miss Robinson won't be here this week, so I'll be your teacher."

He stopped, and patted his thick curly hair. There was an unnatural silence in the room.

"I'd like to get a few things straight," boomed Mr Stone. "I expect the children I teach to work in silence. There are four things I won't have in my classroom: chewing, chattering, passing notes – and, above all, *no laughing*. Is that clear?"

He stopped to pat his head again. Nobody
answered. It wasn't that sort of question. The same
thought was in every child's mind: Come back,
Miss Robinson. Come back *now*!

"Tomorrow we'll be doing Games," said Mr Stone. "And if there's one thing I can't *stand*, it's children who forget their PE shirts or socks or shorts."

His voice dropped to a whisper. "I'll tell you a little secret, boys and girls ..."

He stopped, patted his head, and then bellowed: "I EAT children who forget their PE kit!"

There was a stunned silence. He must be joking, thought Terry. But Mr Stone didn't look like the sort of person who told jokes. He patted his hair again.

"Why does he keep doing that?" Terry whispered to Kevin, who sat next to him.

"What?" whispered Kevin.

"Keep touching his hair like that."

"He's probably like Samson."

"Who?"

"Samson – in the Bible. He was amazingly strong, and the secret of his amazing strength was his hair."

"His hair?"

"Yeah! he was …"

"Who's talking?" bellowed Mr Stone. Without waiting for an answer he pointed at Terry and Kevin. "It was you two. See me at the end of the day for punishment."

Kevin and Terry spent half an hour after school picking up rotting sweet papers and soggy crisp packets which had found their way into the dank corners of the playground.

"Let that be a lesson to you," said Mr Stone, when they'd finished.

"We'd better not forget any of our PE kit tomorrow," said Kevin, as the two boys walked slowly home.

\* \* \* \* \* \* \* \* \* \* \*

"They're not too wet," said Terry. "They'll dry in my bag by the time I get to school."

"Don't be silly," said Mum. "I only took them out of the washing machine five minutes ago."

"But, Mum ..."

"I don't know why you're making such a fuss," said Mum. "Miss Robinson won't mind if you haven't got your shorts this once."

"But it isn't Miss Robinson. It's Mr Stone, and he eats children who forget their PE kit – he said so."

"Don't be silly, Terry. Of course he won't. Now hurry up or you'll be late for school."

Mum marched out of the room clutching the washing basket with the wet shorts.

"What can I do?" thought Terry. "I know Mr Stone won't really eat me, but … If only I had a second pair of shorts, I could …"

Then Terry remembered the old trunk in the attic; the trunk that had once contained the magician's hat out of which Terry's pet rabbits had hopped.

Terry ran as fast as he could to the little room at the top of the hotel. As before, the room was empty except for a large, old-fashioned wardrobe. And at the bottom of the wardrobe was the trunk with the warning label:

Lost property: handle with the greatest care

At the bottom of the trunk, were the leopard-skin shorts which Terry remembered seeing the last time he'd opened the trunk.

Sewn into the waistband of the shorts was an old label which read:

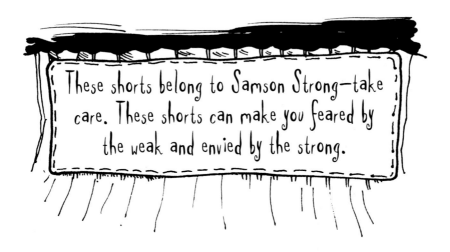

These shorts belong to Samson Strong—take care. These shorts can make you feared by the weak and envied by the strong.

But Terry was in such a hurry that he didn't bother to read the old-fashioned spidery writing. He stuffed the shorts into his school bag and ran out of the room.

\* \* \* \* \* \* \* \* \* \* \*

"What do you call these?" bellowed Mr Stone.

"Err … my shorts," replied Terry.

"Who do you think you are?" asked Mr Stone, holding up the shorts, "Tarzan?"

He laughed very loudly. Several of the children joined in, nervously.

"I suppose I'll have to allow it this time, but no more fancy shorts in future – understood?"

"Yes, Mr Stone."

"OK, everybody," bellowed Mr Stone. "You've got two minutes to get changed and out to the sports field. Ready … Steady … GO!"

Terry pulled on the leopard-skin shorts. They fell down immediately. They were enormous. He pulled the belt from his trousers.

As he hitched the shorts up with the belt, Terry felt a strange tingling in his arms and legs.

"Come on! Hurry up!" shouted Mr Stone. "Last one out closes the door."

Terry pulled the door shut. There was a dramatic slam. The floor and wall of the corridor seem to tremble. Terry looked down at his hand. Gripped in his fist was the door handle. It had snapped off.

"I'm sorry, Mr Stone. I didn't mean to …"

"Hmmmph," said Mr Stone. He bent over and stared at the snapped fitting in the door. "I don't suppose it was your fault, Terry. It must have been rusted or something. You'd have to be Superman to pull the handle off a door. Go and join the others in the hall."

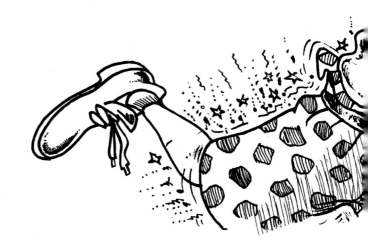

Mr Stone lined the children up in two rows facing each other.

"Today we're going to play basketball," said Mr Stone. He patted his hair.

There was a murmur of excitement.

"First we're going to practise passing, in pairs. I'll show you what I want you to do. Terry will be my partner."

He bent down and picked up a basketball. He patted his hair once again, then threw the basketball to Terry.

Terry usually found basketballs really heavy; too heavy to throw easily. But this morning the ball felt as if it weighed nothing. There was a strange tingling feeling in his arms.

"Throw the ball back to me, Terry," shouted Mr Stone.

The ball seemed to fly out of Terry's hand. It whistled past Mr Stone's right ear and crashed into the wall at the far end of the room.

"Wait until I'm ready," complained Mr Stone. "I can't be expected to catch it if I'm not ready."

He gave a strange laugh and patted his hair nervously. He threw Terry another ball.

"Not so hard this time, Terry."

Terry felt the strange tingling in his arms again.

"OK, Terry. I'm ready now!"

Once again the ball flew out of Terry's hands. The ball hit Mr Stone so hard in the chest that he sat down on the floor with a loud thump.

"I'm so sorry!" said Terry rushing forward. "Let me help you up …"

He grabbed Mr Stone by the hand and pulled.

Mr Stone didn't stand up, he shot up. He flew over Terry's head, did a neat somersault in the air, and landed with a thud on a stack of gym mats in the corner.

There was second of stunned silence. Then
someone giggled. Someone else pointed.

Terry stared at Mr Stone. Something awful had
happened to him. His head was no longer covered
in thick dark curls. It had turned pink and shiny.
Something that looked like a flattened guinea pig
was lying on the gym floor a few metres from
Mr Stone.

"Oooh, look!" shrieked Melanie Griffiths. "His wig's come off!"

Mr Stone desperately tried to cover his shining head with his hands.

"Go back to the classroom – all of you!" He shrieked. "And get changed."

Ten minutes later, just as Terry was stuffing the leopard-skin shorts back into his bag, Mr Thomas, the headteacher, came into the room. He was carrying a basketball.

"Boys and girls, Mr Stone is – um, unwell. I'll be taking you for the rest of today, and I'm delighted to be able to tell you that Miss Robinson will be back tomorrow. Terry, could I have a word with you in the corridor, please?"

"Don't look so worried, Terry," said Mr Thomas, when they got outside the room. "I've spoken to Mr Stone and he tells me that what happened was an accident. You didn't mean to pull the handle off the classroom door, knock him over and throw him across the hall. But there's one thing I want to check for myself."

He threw the basketball at Terry. The heavy ball banged into Terry's chest. He fumbled and dropped it. He picked it up. No longer did it seem weightless.

"Now throw it to me," said Mr Thomas. "As hard as you can."

Terry threw the ball with all his strength. It landed halfway between Terry and Mr Thomas and trickled along the corridor.

"Was that the best you could do?" asked Mr Thomas.

"Yes," admitted Terry.

"All right," said Mr Thomas. "Back to the classroom, Terry."

The strange tingling – and the strength – had vanished. In fact, Terry hadn't felt strong since taking off the shorts.

"Of course," thought Terry. "They were Samson Strong's shorts. They must be magic – like the top hat. Wow! Now I'll have super strength any time I want, just by putting on the shorts!"

Terry stuffed his hand into his bag. There were his trainers, his socks and his T-shirt, but he couldn't feel the rough fur of the shorts.

Terry pulled open the bag and emptied everything out onto the floor, but the shorts had vanished.